Learning about Percentages at the Mall

Dawn McMillan

First hardcover edition published in 2011 by
Capstone Press
151 Good Counsel Drive, P.O. Box 669, Mankato, Minnesota 56002.
www.capstonepub.com

This book was manufactured with paper containing
at least 10 percent post-consumer waste.

Editorial Credits
Sara Johnson, editor; Dona Herweck Rice, editorial director; Sharon Coan, M.S.Ed., editor-in-chief; Lee Aucoin, creative director; Rachelle Cracchiolo, M.S.Ed., publisher; Gene Bentdahl, designer; Eric Manske, production specialist.

Image Credits
The authors and publisher would like to gratefully credit or acknowledge the following for permission to reproduce copyright material: cover (all) Shutterstock; p.1 Shutterstock; p.4 (left) Shutterstock, (right) Getty Images/George Doyle; p.5 Shutterstock; p.6 (both) Shutterstock; p.7 Baseball Bits cover reproduced with permission of Penguin Group USA; p.8 iStock Photo; p.9 (both) Shutterstock; p.10 (top left & bottom) iStock, (top right) Shutterstock; p.11 Photolibrary.com/David Humphreys; p.12 Photolibrary.com/Coll Fransisco Cruz; p.13 Alamy/Scott Pitts; p.14 Alamy/Terry Harris; p.15 iStock Photo; p.16 Shutterstock; p.17 Alamy/Jeff Greenberg; p.18 Shutterstock; p.19 (all) Shutterstock; p.20 Shutterstock; p.21 (left) Shutterstock; p.21 (right) Baseball Bits cover reproduced with permission of Penguin Group USA; p.22 Alamy/Frances Robert; p.23 Shutterstock; p.24 (both) Shutterstock; p.25 iStock Photo; p.26 (both) Shutterstock; p.27 (top & bottom right) Shutterstock; p.27 (bottom left) Getty Images/George Doyle; pp.28–29 (all) Shutterstock

Library of Congress Cataloging-in-Publication Data
McMillan, Dawn.
  Learning about percentages at the mall / by Dawn McMillan. -- 1st hardcover ed.
     p. cm. -- (Real world math)
  Includes index.
  ISBN 978-1-4296-6614-5 (lib. bdg.)
  1. Ratio and proportion--Juvenile literature. I. Title. II. Series.

QA117.M264 2011
513.2'45--dc22
                         2010044644

Printed in the United States of America in Stevens Point, Wisconsin.
092010   005934WZS11

Table of Contents

Grandpa's Birthday 4

Spending Money 5

The Perfect Present 7

Helping Mom at the Grocery Store 8

Searching the Mall 14

Looking for a Present 17

Some Good Luck 21

A Great Birthday Present 26

Problem-Solving Activity 28

Glossary 30

Index 31

Answer Key 32

Grandpa's Birthday

My grandpa's birthday is next week. He is turning 65 years old. We are having a big party at our house. All Grandpa's friends are coming.

I have been saving my allowance for the last 6 weeks. I want to buy him a good birthday present.

This is my grandpa. I want his birthday to be special.

Spending Money

Each week my mom and dad give me $5.00 spending money. I get another $2.50 if I get all my chores done. That means I earn 50% more money when I do all my chores.

My chores are cleaning my room, making my bed, and walking the dog. I also help Dad wash dishes and clean the kitchen 2 nights a week.

My Allowance

Spending money	$5.00
Cleaning my room	$0.50
Making my bed	$0.50
Walking the dog	$1.00
Wash dishes and clean kitchen	$0.50
Total	$7.50

LET'S EXPLORE MATH

Percent (%) means out of 100. One whole is 100%. Look at the square on the right. It represents 1 whole. The whole is divided into 100 pieces. There are 10 pieces shaded. That means that 10% of the whole is shaded. How many pieces would be shaded to show the following percents:

a. 50%? **b.** 15%? **c.** 90%?

5

I have done all my chores for the past 6 weeks so that I have as much money as possible for Grandpa's present. I spent $2.00 each week from my spending money. That means I have saved $33.00 so far for the present.

My Savings

$5.00 + $2.50 = $7.50 each week

$7.50 x 6 weeks = $45.00 earned

But I spent $2.00 a week.

$2.00 x 6 = $12.00 spent

$45.00 – $12.00 = $33.00 saved for Grandpa's present

The Perfect Present

Last week I saw a baseball book collection at a bookstore in the mall. I know Grandpa would like it. But the whole collection was $49.99. I have not saved that much money.

I am going back to the mall today to have a look around. I hope I find something that Grandpa will like and that I can **afford**.

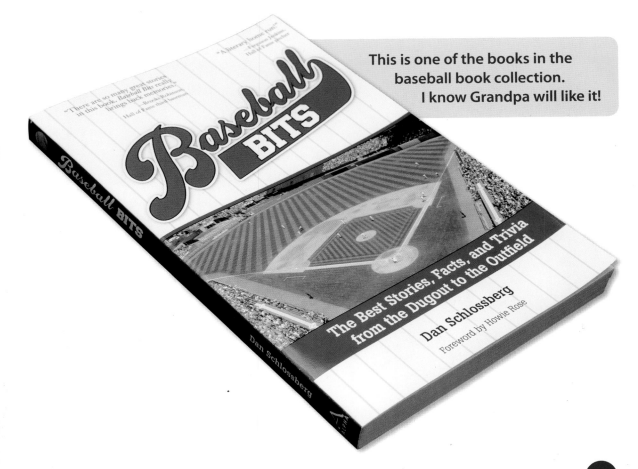

This is one of the books in the baseball book collection. I know Grandpa will like it!

Helping Mom at the Grocery Store

Before I can go look for the present, I need to help Mom with the grocery shopping. We always make a list before we go shopping. And Mom has a weekly **budget** of $150.00. If we see a **bargain**, we grab it! Mom says that I am very good at finding bargains.

Grocery lists can help shoppers stay within their budgets. They are more likely to only buy what is written on the lists.

Right away I see that the pineapples are on sale. Today they are selling for $2.99 each, which is nearly 50% off the regular price. Red apples are also on sale for only $1.99 per pound (0.45 kg). They are even cheaper if you buy a 3 pound (1.4 kg) bag for $4.50.

LET'S EXPLORE MATH

Percentages may be **converted** to fractions and decimals. So 50% is 50 out of 100 or $^{50}/_{100}$ or 0.5. The fraction $^{50}/_{100}$ is the same as $^{5}/_{10}$ or ½. These are known as **equivalent fractions**.

a. Write 25% as a fraction.

b. Write 75% as a decimal.

c. Write 0.4 as a percentage.

d. Write $^{9}/_{10}$ as a percentage and a decimal.

There are other great bargains
at the grocery store today.

cheese block

$1.⁹⁹

SAVE UP TO
PER POUND! **50¢**

carrots

99¢ lb.

BIG SAVINGS!

2 loaves for

$5.⁰⁰

SAVE UP TO **$2.⁹⁸**

There are some **items** that we only buy if they are on sale. Today there is 20% off all candy. My favorite candy is only $2.40. Mom puts a pack into our cart. She says the candy is my **reward** for helping her do the grocery shopping.

Grocery stores have various items on sale every week.

Mom always pays for the groceries with cash. We **estimate** the total grocery bill as we shop so that we will have enough money at the checkout counter. We estimated that the groceries would cost about $130.00. Sure enough, the groceries cost $127.02.

Careful shopping saves money.

LET'S EXPLORE MATH

A grocery store has a sale on fruit. Most days apples and oranges both sell for $2.00 a kilogram. Today they are both selling at 25% off. There is 10% off mangoes, which usually cost $3.00 each.

To figure out how much each item will cost, find the amount of each discount. Then subtract that amount from the usual price. For example, a watermelon costs $2.00. It has a sale sticker that says 10% off. 10% is 0.10, so 0.10 of $2.00 is $0.20. $2.00 − $0.20 = $1.80. The watermelon costs $1.80.

How much would it cost you to buy the items listed below? *Hint*: 25% = 0.25; 10% = 0.10

a. 1 kilogram of apples

c. 3 mangoes

b. 5 kilograms of oranges

Mom gives the **cashier** $150.00. The cashier gives Mom $22.98 in change. A person from the grocery store helps us load all our bags into the car.

The grocery shopping is done. Now Mom and I can go to the mall to look for Grandpa's present. I have a few good ideas.

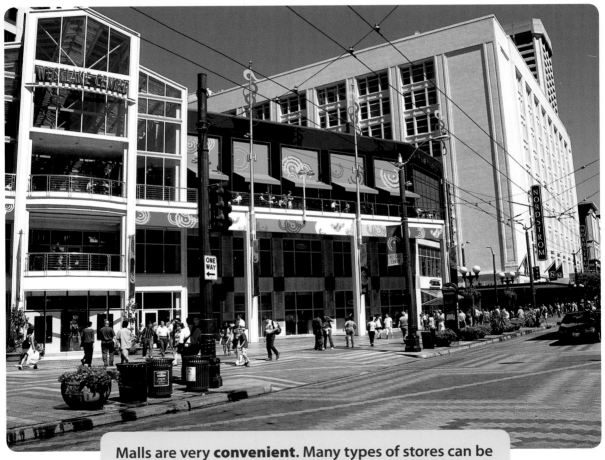

Malls are very **convenient**. Many types of stores can be found under one roof! This can save time for shoppers. They do not have to travel far to buy various items.

Searching the Mall

There are more than 100 stores in the mall near our house. There are bookstores, sports stores, clothing stores, and shoe stores. There are also specialty and furniture stores. There are even outdoor supplies stores. I will be able to find a present for Grandpa in one of these stores!

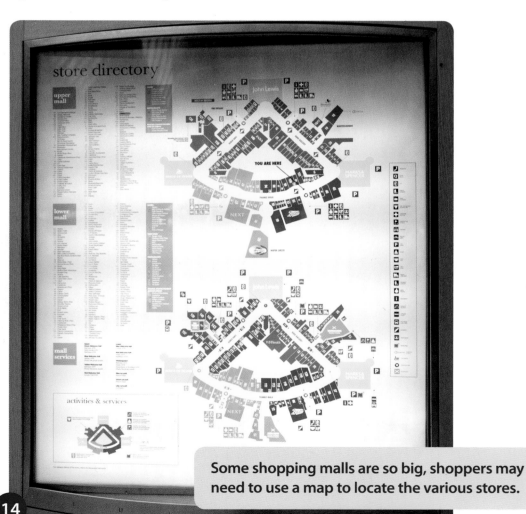

Some shopping malls are so big, shoppers may need to use a map to locate the various stores.

I am not going to find a present for Grandpa at a furniture store, but Mom stops to look through the window. There is an amazing antique couch at 50% off—the original price was $199.00.

"Come on, Mom!" I say as I pull her away. "We are looking for a present for Grandpa!"

Mom calculated the sale price of the couch—50% off $199. First she rounded up the old price of $199 to $200. Then she figured out that 50% or ½ of $200 is $100. The sale price of the couch is about $100.

We walk into a clothing store. Mom says, "What about socks for Grandpa? Look, you can buy two pairs for $14.99."

"Socks?" I say. "Boring!"

Mom laughs. "Grandpa would agree," she says.

Although socks may be boring, they are a useful present.

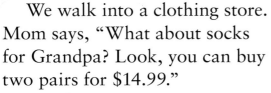

A clothing store is having a huge sale. Many items are greatly reduced.

Sweaters: Retail price $15.00, now 50% off
Sweatpants: Retail price $10.00, now 25% off
T-shirts: Retail price $9.00, now 10% off

a. Calculate the sale price of each item.

b. If you buy 1 of each item, how much money will you save in total?

Looking for a Present

I decide to go to an outdoor supplies store. I will be sure to find something there. Grandpa has a boat and he loves to go fishing. I find the sections of the store where boating and fishing equipment are displayed.

Customers shop in the fishing supplies section of the store.

I find a spotlight for $22.50. There is a set of fish hooks for $29.99. The lifejackets are a bargain—$24.99 each, or 3 for $69.99. But Grandpa has all that fishing gear already.

All boats must carry lifejackets.

Grandpa would like the tackle box, but it costs too much. A fishing **lure** is only $9.99. But I want to spend more than that on Grandpa's present. I see some great **binoculars**, but the cheapest pair is $49.99. That is the same price as the baseball book collection, so I cannot afford to buy binoculars either.

A fishing tackle box

A fishing lure

Binoculars make objects look closer.

I nearly buy Grandpa a new garden hose because it is 50% off. It is reduced from $45.00 to $22.50! I know Grandpa wants a new hose. But I cannot get the baseball book collection out of my mind. A hose is so boring compared to books about baseball!

Even though I am not buying it, I will tell Grandpa about the garden hose. It is half price. What a bargain!

Some Good Luck

"Let's give up for today, Ben," says Mom. "We can come back tomorrow after school."

"OK, Mom," I say. "I wish I could find something as good as that baseball book collection. I know Grandpa will really enjoy reading the first book in the collection."

LET'S EXPLORE MATH

Ben's mom is making candy bags as party favors for Grandpa's birthday. Each bag needs 20 candies. She has 3 bags left to finish filling. What percentage of each bag is filled and what percentage is left to be filled:

a. if there are already 15 candies in 1 bag?

b. if there are already 2 candies in 1 bag?

c. if there are already 10 candies in 1 bag?

Discounts attract many customers.

As we are walking out of the mall, we pass by the bookstore where I saw the baseball book collection. "Mom!" I cry. "Look! There is a big sale going on at the bookstore. They are taking 25% off all books!"

"How much will that baseball book collection cost now?" Mom asks. I sit down on the seat outside the bookstore to figure out the sale price.

First I round up $49.99 to $50.00. To find the discount, I divide $50.00 in half. This shows me that 50% of the book costs $25.00. Next I divide $25.00 in half, so that I get a quarter of $50.00. Now I know that ¼, or 25%, of $50.00 is $12.50. This is the final discount amount. Now to find the sale price, I subtract the discount from the original price: $50.00 − $12.50 = $37.50.

Sale Price of Baseball Books Collection

$49.99 rounded up is $50.00

$50.00 ÷ 2 = $25.00

$25.00 ÷ 2 = $12.50 (discount amount)

$50.00 − $12.50 = $37.50 (sale price)

I realize that I still do not have enough money. Even though I did all my chores for the past 6 weeks, I have only been able to save a total of $33.00.

Mom sees my face and she knows that I am disappointed.

June

S	M	T	W	T	F	S
1	2	3	4	5	6	7
8	9	10	11	12	13	14
15	16	17	18	19	20	2
22	23	24	25	26	27	
29	30					

July

S	M	T	W	T	F	S
		1	2	3	4	5
6	7	8	9	10	11	12
13	14	15	16	17	18	19
20	21	22	23	24	25	26
27	28	29	30	31		

Ben has been saving his allowance for the past 6 weeks.

"Hey, Ben," Mom says, "what if I give you an **advance** on this week's allowance? I'm sure Dad will not mind."

"That would be great! Thanks, Mom!" I say. I give Mom a big hug, right there outside the bookstore.

LET'S EXPLORE MATH

The bookstore is having a huge sale. There is 25% off the retail price of all books. Find the sale prices of the following items. *Hint:* Round the retail price to the nearest dollar.

a. children's paperback book
   retail price: $11.50

b. cookbook
   retail price: $39.99

c. hardback fiction book
   retail price $24. 99

A Great Birthday Present

I add the new figures together. $33.00 + $5.00 = $38.00. That's more than enough! I will even have 50¢ left over.

I am going to use the extra 50¢ to help Mom buy a great birthday card.

$33.00   (allowance saved so far)
+ $5.00   (advance on allowance)
$38.00   (total allowance)

$38.00
− $37.50   (sale price of baseball book collection)
$ 0.50   (money remaining)

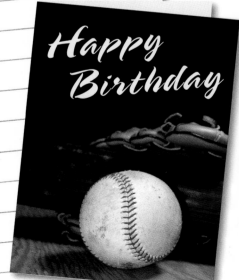

"OK, Mom, I will go into the bookstore to buy Grandpa's birthday present!" I say.

Grandpa is a wonderful grandfather. He deserves a great birthday present. And I think I got him one!

Happy Birthday from ALL of US!

Books at a Bargain

Jamal has a $100.00 gift card to spend at Bargain Books. Jamal loves reading mystery books. But he also likes books about various countries and cultures. And Jamal wants to learn to surf!

Jamal would also like to buy his family some books. His younger sister enjoys adventure stories. His dad enjoys cooking, and his mom loves gardening and fashion. Bargain Books is having a big sale. Jamal has chosen 8 books that he really wants to buy.

MICKEY'S WORLD TRAVEL ADVENTURES
Retail Price: $59.90
Now 25% off

SURFING FOR BEGINNERS
Retail Price: $29.75
Now 20% off

COOKING WITH LOUEY
Retail Price: $48.25
Now 25% off

The Adventures of Pirate Mouse
Retail Price: $19.50
Now 10% off

Retail Price: $35.50
Now ½ price

Retail Price: $16.20
Now 75% off

Retail Price: $22.00
Now ½ price

Retail Price: $42.80
Now 25% off

Solve It!

a. How much money would Jamal spend if he bought all 8 books on sale?

b. Unfortunately, Jamal has only a $100 gift card to spend. Decide which books Jamal would buy if he had to choose, and give reasons for your choices. Think about the books he and his family like.

Use the steps below to help you work out your answers.

Step 1: Round each book price to the nearest dollar.

Step 2: Find the discounted amount for each book.

Step 3: Find the sale price of each book.

Step 4: Calculate the total sale price of all the books.

Step 5: Now decide which books Jamal could buy with his $100.00 gift card. Give reasons for your choices.

Glossary

advance (ad-VANS)—to pay money ahead of time

afford—to have enough money for something

bargain (BAR-guhn)—something bought or sold at a low price

binoculars—a tool for making things look closer

budget (BUHJ-uht)—a plan to work out how much money you earn and spend over a period of time

cashier—a person who takes money and gives change

convenient (kuhn-VEEN-yuhnt)—to be near at hand; to make something easy

converted (kuhn-VERT-uhd)—changed from one form to another

equivalent fractions—fractions that have the same value or amount; fractions that are equal

estimate (ES-tuh-mate)—to calculate something roughly

items—things

lure—something used to attract fish

reward—something given to a person for something done

Index

allowance, 4, 24, 25, 26

bargains, 8, 10, 18, 20

baseball book collection, 7, 19, 20, 21, 23

bill, 12

binoculars, 19

birthday card, 26

boating equipment, 17

bookstores, 14, 22, 23, 25, 27

budget, 8

candy, 11

cash, 12

chores, 5, 6, 24

clothing stores, 14, 16

estimate, 12

fishing, 17, 18, 19

furniture stores, 14, 15

garden hose, 20

grocery shopping, 8–13

mall, 7, 13, 14, 22

outdoor supplies store, 14, 17

price, 19, 25

sale price, 23

sales, 9, 22

savings, 6

shoe stores, 14

specialty stores, 14

spending money, 5, 6

sports stores, 14

Let's Explore Math

Page 5:
a. 50 pieces would be shaded
b. 15 pieces would be shaded
c. 90 pieces would be shaded

Page 9:
a. $25\% = \frac{25}{100}$ or $\frac{1}{4}$ c. $0.4 = 40\%$
b. $75\% = 0.75$ d. $\frac{9}{10} = 90\%$ and 0.9

Page 12:
a. 25% = 0.25, so 0.25 of $2.00 = $0.50.
$2.00 − $0.50 = $1.50 for 1 kg of apples
b. 25% = 0.25, so 0.25 of $2.00 = $0.50.
$2.00 − $0.50 = $1.50
$1.50 x 5 = $7.50 for 5 kg of oranges
c. 10% = 0.10, so 0.10 of $3.00 = $0.30.
$3.00 − $0.30 = $2.70 for 1 mango
$2.70 x 3 = $8.10. So 3 mangoes = $8.10

Page 16:
a. sweater: 0.5 of $15.00 = $7.50
$15.00 − $7.50 = $7.50 sale price
sweatpants: 0.25 of $10.00 = $2.50
$10.00 − $2.50 = $7.50 sale price
T-shirt: 0.10 of $9.00 = $0.90
$9.00 − $0.90 = $8.10 sale price
b. original total: $15.00 + $10.00 + $9.00
= $34.00
sale total: $7.50 + $7.50 + $8.10 = $23.10
$34.00 − $23.10 = $10.90 savings

Page 21:
a. $\frac{15}{20} = \frac{3}{4} = 75\%$ is already filled
100% − 75% = 25% is left to be filled
b. $\frac{2}{20} = \frac{1}{10} = 10\%$ is already filled
100% − 10% = 90% is left to be filled
c. $\frac{10}{20} = \frac{1}{2} = 50\%$ is already filled
100% − 50% = 50% is left to be filled

Page 25:
a. $11.50 = $12.00 rounded up
25% = 0.25, so 0.25 of $12.00 = $3.00.
$12.00 − $3.00 = $9.00 sale price
b. $39.99 = $40.00 rounded up
25% = 0.25, so 0.25 of $40.00 = $10.00.
$40.00 − $10.00 = $30.00 sale price
c. $24.99 = $25.00 rounded up
25% = 0.25, so 0.25 of $25.00 = $6.25.
$25.00 − $6.25 = $18.75 sale price

Pages 28–29:

Problem-Solving Activity

a. *Mickey's World Travel Adventures*
25% of $60.00 = $15.00 discounted amount
$60.00 − $15.00 = $45.00 sale price

Surfing for Beginners
20% of $30.00 = $6.00 discounted amount
$30.00 − $6.00 = $24.00 sale price

Cooking with Louey
25% of $48.00 = $12.00 discounted amount
$48.00 − $12.00 = $36.00 sale price

The Adventures of Pirate Mouse
10% of $20.00 = $2.00 discounted amount
$20.00 − $2.00 = $18.00 sale price

Exploring France
50% of $36.00 = $18.00 discounted amount
$36.00 − $18.00 = $18.00 sale price

Mystery of the Cherry Orchard
75% of $16.00 = $12.00 discounted amount
$16.00 − $12.00 = $4.00 sale price

Green Thumbs Gardening
50% of $22.00 = $11.00 discounted amount
$22.00 − $11.00 = $11.00 sale price

Fashion Designing
25% of $43.00 = $10.75 discounted amount
$43.00 − $10.75 = $32.25 sale price

Total sale price of all 8 books:
$45.00 + $24.00 + $36.00 + $18.00 + $18.00
+ $4.00 + $11.00 + $32.25 = $188.25
Jamal would spend $188.25.

b. Answers will vary.